50 Homemade Fermented Hot Sauce Recipes for Home

By: Kelly Johnson

Table of Contents

- Fermented Watermelon Hot Sauce
- Fermented Avocado and Jalapeno Hot Sauce
- Fermented Pineapple and Papaya Hot Sauce
- Fermented Cranberry and Jalapeno Hot Sauce
- Fermented Mango and Pineapple Hot Sauce
- Fermented Strawberry and Habanero Hot Sauce
- Fermented Tomato and Basil Hot Sauce
- Fermented Grapefruit and Ghost Pepper Hot Sauce
- Fermented Pineapple and Mango Hot Sauce
- Fermented Kiwi and Jalapeno Hot Sauce
- Fermented Cherry and Ghost Pepper Hot Sauce
- Fermented Blackberry and Habanero Hot Sauce
- Fermented Raspberry and Jalapeno Hot Sauce
- Fermented Apple and Cayenne Hot Sauce
- Fermented Plum and Scotch Bonnet Hot Sauce

Classic Fermented Cayenne Hot Sauce

Ingredients:

- 1 pound fresh cayenne peppers
- 4 cloves garlic, minced
- 2 tablespoons sea salt
- 2 cups filtered water

Instructions:

Wash the cayenne peppers thoroughly and remove the stems.
Slice the peppers into small pieces and place them in a clean glass jar or fermentation crock.
Add minced garlic on top of the peppers.
Dissolve sea salt in filtered water to create a brine solution.
Pour the brine solution over the peppers until they are fully submerged.
Place a fermentation weight on top to keep the peppers submerged under the brine.
Cover the jar with a lid or cloth secured with a rubber band to keep out dust and insects.
Allow the mixture to ferment at room temperature, away from direct sunlight, for about 1-2 weeks. Check the fermentation progress daily.
After fermentation, blend the mixture until smooth using a blender or food processor.
If the sauce is too thick, you can strain it through a fine-mesh sieve to achieve desired consistency.
Transfer the fermented hot sauce into clean glass bottles or jars for storage.
Store the hot sauce in the refrigerator. It will continue to ferment slowly, developing more flavor over time.

Enjoy your homemade Classic Fermented Cayenne Hot Sauce on your favorite dishes! Adjust the amount of garlic or salt according to your taste preferences.

Smoky Chipotle Fermented Hot Sauce

Ingredients:

- 1 pound ripe red jalapeno peppers
- 3-4 chipotle peppers (dried or canned in adobo sauce)
- 4 cloves garlic, minced
- 2 tablespoons sea salt
- 2 cups filtered water

Instructions:

Wash the jalapeno peppers and remove the stems. If using canned chipotle peppers, drain them from the adobo sauce.

Slice the jalapeno peppers in half and remove the seeds and membranes for a milder sauce, or leave them in for extra heat.

Chop the chipotle peppers into smaller pieces.

Place the jalapeno peppers, chipotle peppers, and minced garlic in a clean glass jar or fermentation crock.

Dissolve sea salt in filtered water to create a brine solution.

Pour the brine solution over the peppers until they are fully submerged.

Place a fermentation weight on top to keep the peppers submerged under the brine.

Cover the jar with a lid or cloth secured with a rubber band.

Allow the mixture to ferment at room temperature, away from direct sunlight, for about 1-2 weeks. Check the fermentation progress daily.

After fermentation, blend the mixture until smooth using a blender or food processor.

If the sauce is too thick, you can strain it through a fine-mesh sieve to achieve desired consistency.

Transfer the fermented hot sauce into clean glass bottles or jars for storage.

Store the hot sauce in the refrigerator. It will continue to ferment slowly, developing more flavor over time.

Enjoy the smoky, spicy flavor of your homemade Smoky Chipotle Fermented Hot Sauce on tacos, grilled meats, or any dish that could use a kick of heat! Adjust the amount of chipotle peppers to your preferred level of smokiness and heat.

Garlic and Jalapeno Fermented Hot Sauce

Ingredients:

- 1 pound fresh jalapeno peppers
- 6 cloves garlic, minced
- 2 tablespoons sea salt
- 2 cups filtered water

Instructions:

Wash the jalapeno peppers thoroughly and remove the stems.
Slice the jalapeno peppers into small pieces and place them in a clean glass jar or fermentation crock.
Add minced garlic on top of the peppers.
Dissolve sea salt in filtered water to create a brine solution.
Pour the brine solution over the peppers until they are fully submerged.
Place a fermentation weight on top to keep the peppers submerged under the brine.
Cover the jar with a lid or cloth secured with a rubber band to keep out dust and insects.
Allow the mixture to ferment at room temperature, away from direct sunlight, for about 1-2 weeks. Check the fermentation progress daily.
After fermentation, blend the mixture until smooth using a blender or food processor.
If the sauce is too thick, you can strain it through a fine-mesh sieve to achieve desired consistency.
Transfer the fermented hot sauce into clean glass bottles or jars for storage.
Store the hot sauce in the refrigerator. It will continue to ferment slowly, developing more flavor over time.

Enjoy the flavorful combination of garlic and jalapeno in your homemade Fermented Hot Sauce! Adjust the amount of garlic or jalapeno peppers according to your taste preferences.

Pineapple and Scotch Bonnet Hot Sauce

Ingredients:

- 1 pound Scotch Bonnet peppers
- 2 cups pineapple chunks
- 4 cloves garlic, minced
- 2 tablespoons sea salt
- 2 cups filtered water

Instructions:

Wash the Scotch Bonnet peppers and remove the stems. Wear gloves to protect your hands from the spicy oils.

Slice the Scotch Bonnet peppers in half and remove the seeds and membranes for a milder sauce, or leave them in for extra heat.

Peel and chop the pineapple into chunks.

Place the Scotch Bonnet peppers, pineapple chunks, and minced garlic in a clean glass jar or fermentation crock.

Dissolve sea salt in filtered water to create a brine solution.

Pour the brine solution over the peppers and pineapple until they are fully submerged.

Place a fermentation weight on top to keep the ingredients submerged under the brine.

Cover the jar with a lid or cloth secured with a rubber band to keep out dust and insects.

Allow the mixture to ferment at room temperature, away from direct sunlight, for about 1-2 weeks. Check the fermentation progress daily.

After fermentation, blend the mixture until smooth using a blender or food processor.

If the sauce is too thick, you can strain it through a fine-mesh sieve to achieve desired consistency.

Transfer the fermented hot sauce into clean glass bottles or jars for storage.

Store the hot sauce in the refrigerator. It will continue to ferment slowly, developing more flavor over time.

Enjoy the sweet and spicy combination of pineapple and Scotch Bonnet peppers in your homemade Fermented Hot Sauce! Adjust the amount of peppers or pineapple according to your taste preferences.

Fermented Sriracha Hot Sauce

Ingredients:

- 2 pounds red jalapeno peppers
- 4 cloves garlic, minced
- 2 tablespoons brown sugar
- 2 tablespoons sea salt
- 1 tablespoon fish sauce (optional)
- 2 cups filtered water

Instructions:

Wash the red jalapeno peppers thoroughly and remove the stems.
Slice the jalapeno peppers in half and remove the seeds and membranes for a milder sauce, or leave them in for extra heat.
Place the jalapeno peppers and minced garlic in a clean glass jar or fermentation crock.
Dissolve brown sugar and sea salt in filtered water to create a brine solution.
Pour the brine solution over the peppers until they are fully submerged.
If using fish sauce, add it to the brine solution and mix well.
Place a fermentation weight on top to keep the peppers submerged under the brine.
Cover the jar with a lid or cloth secured with a rubber band to keep out dust and insects.
Allow the mixture to ferment at room temperature, away from direct sunlight, for about 1-2 weeks. Check the fermentation progress daily.
After fermentation, blend the mixture until smooth using a blender or food processor.
If the sauce is too thick, you can strain it through a fine-mesh sieve to achieve desired consistency.
Transfer the fermented hot sauce into clean glass bottles or jars for storage.
Store the hot sauce in the refrigerator. It will continue to ferment slowly, developing more flavor over time.

Enjoy the tangy and spicy flavor of your homemade Fermented Sriracha Hot Sauce!
Adjust the amount of garlic, sugar, or fish sauce according to your taste preferences.

Spicy Ghost Pepper Fermented Hot Sauce

Ingredients:

- 1/2 pound ghost peppers (also known as Bhut Jolokia)
- 4 cloves garlic, minced
- 2 tablespoons brown sugar
- 2 tablespoons sea salt
- 2 cups filtered water

Instructions:

Wear gloves when handling ghost peppers to protect your skin from the intense heat.
Wash the ghost peppers thoroughly and remove the stems.
Slice the ghost peppers in half and remove the seeds and membranes for a milder sauce, or leave them in for extra heat.
Place the ghost peppers and minced garlic in a clean glass jar or fermentation crock.
Dissolve brown sugar and sea salt in filtered water to create a brine solution.
Pour the brine solution over the peppers until they are fully submerged.
Place a fermentation weight on top to keep the peppers submerged under the brine.
Cover the jar with a lid or cloth secured with a rubber band to keep out dust and insects.
Allow the mixture to ferment at room temperature, away from direct sunlight, for about 1-2 weeks. Check the fermentation progress daily.
After fermentation, blend the mixture until smooth using a blender or food processor.
If the sauce is too thick, you can strain it through a fine-mesh sieve to achieve desired consistency.
Transfer the fermented hot sauce into clean glass bottles or jars for storage.
Store the hot sauce in the refrigerator. It will continue to ferment slowly, developing more flavor over time.

Enjoy the fiery heat of your homemade Spicy Ghost Pepper Fermented Hot Sauce!

Adjust the amount of garlic, sugar, or salt according to your taste preferences.

Apple Cider Vinegar Fermented Hot Sauce

Ingredients:

- 1 pound hot peppers (such as jalapeno, serrano, or habanero), stemmed and halved
- 4 cloves garlic, peeled
- 1 tablespoon sea salt
- 2 cups filtered water
- 1/4 cup raw, unfiltered apple cider vinegar

Instructions:

In a clean glass jar or fermentation crock, combine the halved hot peppers and garlic cloves.

Dissolve the sea salt in filtered water to create a brine solution.

Pour the brine solution over the peppers and garlic until they are fully submerged. Ensure there's at least an inch of space between the top of the mixture and the rim of the jar.

Place a fermentation weight on top of the peppers and garlic to keep them submerged under the brine.

Cover the jar with a lid or a cloth secured with a rubber band to allow gases to escape whlle preventing dust and insects from entering.

Place the jar in a cool, dark area away from direct sunlight and let it ferment for about 1-2 weeks. Check the fermentation progress daily and skim off any mold that may form on the surface.

Once the fermentation is complete and the peppers have softened, transfer the contents of the jar to a blender or food processor.

Add the apple cider vinegar to the blender or food processor and blend until smooth.

If the sauce is too thick, you can add a bit of filtered water or more apple cider vinegar to reach your desired consistency.

Strain the blended mixture through a fine-mesh sieve to remove any solids, if desired.

Transfer the strained hot sauce to clean glass bottles or jars for storage.

Seal the bottles or jars and store the hot sauce in the refrigerator. It will continue to ferment slowly, developing more flavor over time.

Enjoy the tangy and spicy kick of your homemade Apple Cider Vinegar Fermented Hot Sauce! Adjust the type and amount of hot peppers used according to your preferred level of heat.

Fermented Serrano and Lime Hot Sauce

Ingredients:

- 1 pound serrano peppers, stemmed
- Zest and juice of 2 limes
- 4 cloves garlic, peeled
- 1 tablespoon sea salt
- 2 cups filtered water

Instructions:

Wash the serrano peppers thoroughly and remove the stems.

In a clean glass jar or fermentation crock, combine the serrano peppers, lime zest, lime juice, and garlic cloves.

Dissolve the sea salt in filtered water to create a brine solution.

Pour the brine solution over the peppers, lime zest, lime juice, and garlic until they are fully submerged. Leave about an inch of headspace at the top of the jar.

Place a fermentation weight on top of the peppers to keep them submerged under the brine.

Cover the jar with a lid or a cloth secured with a rubber band to allow gases to escape while preventing dust and insects from entering.

Place the jar in a cool, dark area away from direct sunlight and let it ferment for about 1-2 weeks. Check the fermentation progress daily and skim off any mold that may form on the surface.

Once the fermentation is complete and the peppers have softened, transfer the contents of the jar to a blender or food processor.

Blend the mixture until smooth.

If the sauce is too thick, you can add a bit of filtered water to reach your desired consistency.

Strain the blended mixture through a fine-mesh sieve to remove any solids, if desired.

Transfer the strained hot sauce to clean glass bottles or jars for storage.

Seal the bottles or jars and store the hot sauce in the refrigerator. It will continue to ferment slowly, developing more flavor over time.

Enjoy the zesty and spicy flavor of your homemade Fermented Serrano and Lime Hot Sauce! Adjust the amount of lime zest or juice according to your taste preferences.

Ginger and Turmeric Fermented Hot Sauce

Ingredients:

- 1 pound hot peppers (such as jalapeno, serrano, or habanero), stemmed and halved
- 2 tablespoons grated fresh ginger
- 2 tablespoons grated fresh turmeric (or 2 teaspoons ground turmeric)
- 4 cloves garlic, peeled
- 1 tablespoon sea salt
- 2 cups filtered water

Instructions:

In a clean glass jar or fermentation crock, combine the halved hot peppers, grated ginger, grated turmeric, and garlic cloves.

Dissolve the sea salt in filtered water to create a brine solution.

Pour the brine solution over the peppers, ginger, turmeric, and garlic until they are fully submerged. Ensure there's at least an inch of space between the top of the mixture and the rim of the jar.

Place a fermentation weight on top of the peppers to keep them submerged under the brine.

Cover the jar with a lid or a cloth secured with a rubber band to allow gases to escape while preventing dust and insects from entering.

Place the jar in a cool, dark area away from direct sunlight and let it ferment for about 1-2 weeks. Check the fermentation progress daily and skim off any mold that may form on the surface.

Once the fermentation is complete and the peppers have softened, transfer the contents of the jar to a blender or food processor.

Blend the mixture until smooth.

If the sauce is too thick, you can add a bit of filtered water to reach your desired consistency.

Strain the blended mixture through a fine-mesh sieve to remove any solids, if desired.

Transfer the strained hot sauce to clean glass bottles or jars for storage.

Seal the bottles or jars and store the hot sauce in the refrigerator. It will continue to ferment slowly, developing more flavor over time.

Enjoy the vibrant flavor and health benefits of your homemade Ginger and Turmeric Fermented Hot Sauce! Adjust the amount of ginger or turmeric according to your taste preferences.

Korean Gochujang-style Fermented Hot Sauce

Ingredients:

- 1 pound Korean red chili peppers (gochugaru), stemmed
- 4 cloves garlic, minced
- 2 tablespoons glutinous rice powder (or rice flour)
- 1 tablespoon brown sugar
- 1 tablespoon soy sauce
- 1 tablespoon fish sauce (optional)
- 2 cups filtered water

Instructions:

In a bowl, mix the glutinous rice powder with a small amount of filtered water to form a smooth paste.

In a saucepan, combine the remaining filtered water and brown sugar. Heat over medium heat until the sugar dissolves completely.

Add the rice paste to the saucepan and stir continuously until the mixture thickens slightly.

Remove the saucepan from heat and let the mixture cool to room temperature.

In a clean glass jar or fermentation crock, combine the Korean red chili peppers, minced garlic, soy sauce, and fish sauce (if using).

Pour the cooled rice paste mixture over the pepper mixture in the jar.

Using clean hands or a utensil, mix everything together thoroughly until well combined.

Ensure the peppers are fully submerged under the liquid. If necessary, add more filtered water to cover the peppers completely.

Place a fermentation weight on top of the peppers to keep them submerged under the liquid.

Cover the jar with a lid or a cloth secured with a rubber band to allow gases to escape while preventing dust and insects from entering.

Place the jar in a cool, dark area away from direct sunlight and let it ferment for about 1-2 weeks. Check the fermentation progress daily and skim off any mold that may form on the surface.

Once the fermentation is complete and the flavors have developed, transfer the contents of the jar to a blender or food processor.

Blend the mixture until smooth.

Strain the blended mixture through a fine-mesh sieve to remove any solids, if
desired.
Transfer the strained hot sauce to clean glass bottles or jars for storage.
Seal the bottles or jars and store the hot sauce in the refrigerator. It will continue
to ferment slowly, developing more flavor over time.

Enjoy the bold and savory flavor of your homemade Korean Gochujang-style Fermented
Hot Sauce! Adjust the amount of garlic, soy sauce, or fish sauce according to your taste
preferences.

Fermented Thai Chili Hot Sauce

Ingredients:

- 1 pound Thai chili peppers
- 4 cloves garlic, minced
- 1 tablespoon palm sugar (or brown sugar)
- 1 tablespoon sea salt
- 2 cups filtered water

Instructions:

Wash the Thai chili peppers thoroughly and remove the stems.

In a clean glass jar or fermentation crock, combine the Thai chili peppers and minced garlic.

Dissolve palm sugar and sea salt in filtered water to create a brine solution.

Pour the brine solution over the peppers and garlic until they are fully submerged. Leave about an inch of headspace at the top of the jar.

Place a fermentation weight on top of the peppers to keep them submerged under the brine.

Cover the jar with a lid or a cloth secured with a rubber band to allow gases to escape while preventing dust and insects from entering.

Place the jar in a cool, dark area away from direct sunlight and let it ferment for about 1-2 weeks. Check the fermentation progress daily and skim off any mold that may form on the surface.

Once the fermentation is complete and the peppers have softened, transfer the contents of the jar to a blender or food processor.

Blend the mixture until smooth.

Strain the blended mixture through a fine-mesh sieve to remove any solids, if desired.

Transfer the strained hot sauce to clean glass bottles or jars for storage.

Seal the bottles or jars and store the hot sauce in the refrigerator. It will continue to ferment slowly, developing more flavor over time.

Enjoy the vibrant and spicy flavor of your homemade Fermented Thai Chili Hot Sauce!

Adjust the amount of garlic, sugar, or salt according to your taste preferences.

Roasted Red Pepper Fermented Hot Sauce

Ingredients:

- 1 pound red bell peppers
- 2 cloves garlic, minced
- 2 tablespoons sea salt
- 2 cups filtered water

Instructions:

Preheat your oven to 400°F (200°C).
Wash the red bell peppers and pat them dry with a paper towel. Cut the peppers in half and remove the seeds and membranes.
Place the pepper halves on a baking sheet, skin side up, and roast them in the preheated oven for about 20-25 minutes, or until the skins are blistered and charred.
Remove the peppers from the oven and transfer them to a bowl. Cover the bowl with plastic wrap and let the peppers steam for about 10 minutes.
Once cooled, peel off the skins from the peppers and discard them.
In a clean glass jar or fermentation crock, combine the roasted red peppers and minced garlic.
Dissolve sea salt in filtered water to create a brine solution.
Pour the brine solution over the peppers until they are fully submerged. Leave about an inch of headspace at the top of the jar.
Place a fermentation weight on top of the peppers to keep them submerged under the brine.
Cover the jar with a lid or a cloth secured with a rubber band to allow gases to escape while preventing dust and insects from entering.
Place the jar in a cool, dark area away from direct sunlight and let it ferment for about 1-2 weeks. Check the fermentation progress daily and skim off any mold that may form on the surface.
Once the fermentation is complete, transfer the contents of the jar to a blender or food processor.
Blend the mixture until smooth.
Strain the blended mixture through a fine-mesh sieve to remove any solids, if desired.
Transfer the strained hot sauce to clean glass bottles or jars for storage.

Seal the bottles or jars and store the hot sauce in the refrigerator. It will continue to ferment slowly, developing more flavor over time.

Enjoy the smoky and savory flavor of your homemade Roasted Red Pepper Fermented Hot Sauce! Adjust the amount of garlic or salt according to your taste preferences.

Fermented Green Chili Hot Sauce

Ingredients:

- 1 pound green chili peppers (such as jalapenos or serranos), stemmed
- 4 cloves garlic, peeled
- 1 tablespoon sea salt
- 2 cups filtered water

Instructions:

Wash the green chili peppers thoroughly and remove the stems.
In a clean glass jar or fermentation crock, combine the green chili peppers and garlic cloves.
Dissolve sea salt in filtered water to create a brine solution.
Pour the brine solution over the peppers and garlic until they are fully submerged.
Ensure there's at least an inch of space between the top of the mixture and the rim of the jar.
Place a fermentation weight on top of the peppers to keep them submerged under the brine.
Cover the jar with a lid or a cloth secured with a rubber band to allow gases to escape while preventing dust and insects from entering.
Place the jar in a cool, dark area away from direct sunlight and let it ferment for about 1-2 weeks. Check the fermentation progress daily and skim off any mold that may form on the surface.
Once the fermentation is complete and the peppers have softened, transfer the contents of the jar to a blender or food processor.
Blend the mixture until smooth.
Strain the blended mixture through a fine-mesh sieve to remove any solids, if desired.
Transfer the strained hot sauce to clean glass bottles or jars for storage.
Seal the bottles or jars and store the hot sauce in the refrigerator. It will continue to ferment slowly, developing more flavor over time.

Enjoy the tangy and spicy flavor of your homemade Fermented Green Chili Hot Sauce! Adjust the amount of garlic or salt according to your taste preferences. You can also experiment with adding other ingredients like lime juice or cilantro for extra flavor.

Tomato and Basil Fermented Hot Sauce

Ingredients:

- 2 pounds ripe tomatoes, diced
- 1 cup fresh basil leaves
- 4 cloves garlic, minced
- 1 tablespoon sea salt
- 2 cups filtered water

Instructions:

In a clean glass jar or fermentation crock, layer the diced tomatoes, basil leaves, and minced garlic.

Dissolve sea salt in filtered water to create a brine solution.

Pour the brine solution over the tomatoes, basil, and garlic until they are fully submerged. Ensure there's at least an inch of space between the top of the mixture and the rim of the jar.

Place a fermentation weight on top to keep the ingredients submerged under the brine.

Cover the jar with a lid or a cloth secured with a rubber band to allow gases to escape while preventing dust and insects from entering.

Place the jar in a cool, dark area away from direct sunlight and let it ferment for about 1-2 weeks. Check the fermentation progress daily and skim off any mold that may form on the surface.

Once the fermentation is complete and the flavors have developed, transfer the contents of the jar to a blender or food processor.

Blend the mixture until smooth.

Strain the blended mixture through a fine-mesh sieve to remove any solids, if desired.

Transfer the strained hot sauce to clean glass bottles or jars for storage.

Seal the bottles or jars and store the hot sauce in the refrigerator. It will continue to ferment slowly, developing more flavor over time.

Enjoy the rich and flavorful taste of your homemade Tomato and Basil Fermented Hot Sauce! Adjust the amount of garlic or basil according to your taste preferences. You can also add other herbs or spices for additional flavor complexity.

Mango and Lime Fermented Hot Sauce

Ingredients:

- 2 ripe mangoes, peeled and diced
- Zest and juice of 2 limes
- 4 cloves garlic, minced
- 1 tablespoon sea salt
- 2 cups filtered water
- 1-2 habanero peppers, stemmed and halved (optional, for extra heat)

Instructions:

In a clean glass jar or fermentation crock, combine the diced mangoes, lime zest, lime juice, minced garlic, and habanero peppers (if using).

Dissolve sea salt in filtered water to create a brine solution.

Pour the brine solution over the mango mixture until it is fully submerged. Ensure there's at least an inch of space between the top of the mixture and the rim of the jar.

Place a fermentation weight on top to keep the ingredients submerged under the brine.

Cover the jar with a lid or a cloth secured with a rubber band to allow gases to escape while preventing dust and insects from entering.

Place the jar in a cool, dark area away from direct sunlight and let it ferment for about 1-2 weeks. Check the fermentation progress daily and skim off any mold that may form on the surface.

Once the fermentation is complete and the flavors have developed, transfer the contents of the jar to a blender or food processor.

Blend the mixture until smooth.

Strain the blended mixture through a fine-mesh sieve to remove any solids, if desired.

Transfer the strained hot sauce to clean glass bottles or jars for storage.

Seal the bottles or jars and store the hot sauce in the refrigerator. It will continue to ferment slowly, developing more flavor over time.

Enjoy the sweet, tangy, and spicy flavor of your homemade Mango and Lime Fermented Hot Sauce! Adjust the amount of garlic, habanero peppers, or lime according to your taste preferences.

Fermented Carolina Reaper Hot Sauce

Ingredients:

- 1/2 pound Carolina Reaper peppers, stemmed
- 4 cloves garlic, peeled
- 1 tablespoon brown sugar
- 1 tablespoon sea salt
- 2 cups filtered water

Instructions:

Wear gloves when handling Carolina Reaper peppers to avoid skin irritation from their intense heat.

Wash the Carolina Reaper peppers thoroughly and remove the stems.

In a clean glass jar or fermentation crock, combine the Carolina Reaper peppers and garlic cloves.

Dissolve brown sugar and sea salt in filtered water to create a brine solution.

Pour the brine solution over the peppers and garlic until they are fully submerged. Leave about an inch of headspace at the top of the jar.

Place a fermentation weight on top of the peppers to keep them submerged under the brine.

Cover the jar with a lid or a cloth secured with a rubber band to allow gases to escape while preventing dust and insects from entering.

Place the jar in a cool, dark area away from direct sunlight and let it ferment for about 1-2 weeks. Check the fermentation progress daily and skim off any mold that may form on the surface.

Once the fermentation is complete and the peppers have softened, transfer the contents of the jar to a blender or food processor.

Blend the mixture until smooth.

Strain the blended mixture through a fine-mesh sieve to remove any solids, if desired.

Transfer the strained hot sauce to clean glass bottles or jars for storage.

Seal the bottles or jars and store the hot sauce in the refrigerator. It will continue to ferment slowly, developing more flavor over time.

Enjoy the intense heat of your homemade Fermented Carolina Reaper Hot Sauce! Adjust the amount of garlic, sugar, or salt according to your taste preferences.

Cilantro and Lime Fermented Hot Sauce

Ingredients:

- 1 pound hot peppers (such as jalapeno or serrano), stemmed
- 1 cup fresh cilantro leaves
- Zest and juice of 2 limes
- 4 cloves garlic, peeled
- 1 tablespoon sea salt
- 2 cups filtered water

Instructions:

Wash the hot peppers thoroughly and remove the stems.
In a clean glass jar or fermentation crock, combine the hot peppers, cilantro leaves, lime zest, lime juice, and garlic cloves.
Dissolve sea salt in filtered water to create a brine solution.
Pour the brine solution over the pepper mixture until they are fully submerged. Ensure there's at least an inch of space between the top of the mixture and the rim of the jar.
Place a fermentation weight on top of the mixture to keep everything submerged under the brine.
Cover the jar with a lid or a cloth secured with a rubber band to allow gases to escape while preventing dust and insects from entering.
Place the jar in a cool, dark area away from direct sunlight and let it ferment for about 1-2 weeks. Check the fermentation progress daily and skim off any mold that may form on the surface.
Once the fermentation is complete and the peppers have softened, transfer the contents of the jar to a blender or food processor.
Blend the mixture until smooth.
Strain the blended mixture through a fine-mesh sieve to remove any solids, if desired.
Transfer the strained hot sauce to clean glass bottles or jars for storage.
Seal the bottles or jars and store the hot sauce in the refrigerator. It will continue to ferment slowly, developing more flavor over time.

Enjoy the refreshing and spicy flavor of your homemade Cilantro and Lime Fermented Hot Sauce! Adjust the amount of cilantro, lime, or garlic according to your taste preferences.

Fermented Scotch Bonnet and Pineapple Hot Sauce

Ingredients:

- 1 pound Scotch Bonnet peppers, stemmed
- 2 cups fresh pineapple chunks
- 4 cloves garlic, peeled
- 1 tablespoon sea salt
- 2 cups filtered water

Instructions:

Wash the Scotch Bonnet peppers thoroughly and remove the stems.
In a clean glass jar or fermentation crock, combine the Scotch Bonnet peppers, pineapple chunks, and garlic cloves.
Dissolve sea salt in filtered water to create a brine solution.
Pour the brine solution over the pepper and pineapple mixture until they are fully submerged. Ensure there's at least an inch of space between the top of the mixture and the rim of the jar.
Place a fermentation weight on top of the mixture to keep everything submerged under the brine.
Cover the jar with a lid or a cloth secured with a rubber band to allow gases to escape while preventing dust and insects from entering.
Place the jar in a cool, dark area away from direct sunlight and let it ferment for about 1-2 weeks. Check the fermentation progress daily and skim off any mold that may form on the surface.
Once the fermentation is complete and the peppers have softened, transfer the contents of the jar to a blender or food processor.
Blend the mixture until smooth.
Strain the blended mixture through a fine-mesh sieve to remove any solids, if desired.
Transfer the strained hot sauce to clean glass bottles or jars for storage.
Seal the bottles or jars and store the hot sauce in the refrigerator. It will continue to ferment slowly, developing more flavor over time.

Enjoy the sweet and spicy flavor of your homemade Fermented Scotch Bonnet and Pineapple Hot Sauce! Adjust the amount of garlic or pineapple according to your taste preferences.

Fermented Black Garlic Hot Sauce

Ingredients:

- 1 pound hot peppers (such as red jalapenos, habaneros, or Scotch bonnets), stemmed
- 1 cup black garlic cloves (approximately 1 head)
- 4 cloves garlic, peeled
- 1 tablespoon brown sugar
- 1 tablespoon sea salt
- 2 cups filtered water

Instructions:

Wash the hot peppers thoroughly and remove the stems.
In a clean glass jar or fermentation crock, combine the hot peppers, black garlic cloves, and peeled garlic cloves.
Dissolve brown sugar and sea salt in filtered water to create a brine solution.
Pour the brine solution over the pepper and garlic mixture until they are fully submerged. Ensure there's at least an inch of space between the top of the mixture and the rim of the jar.
Place a fermentation weight on top of the mixture to keep everything submerged under the brine.
Cover the jar with a lid or a cloth secured with a rubber band to allow gases to escape while preventing dust and insects from entering.
Place the jar in a cool, dark area away from direct sunlight and let it ferment for about 1-2 weeks. Check the fermentation progress daily and skim off any mold that may form on the surface.
Once the fermentation is complete and the peppers have softened, transfer the contents of the jar to a blender or food processor.
Blend the mixture until smooth.
Strain the blended mixture through a fine-mesh sieve to remove any solids, if desired.
Transfer the strained hot sauce to clean glass bottles or jars for storage.
Seal the bottles or jars and store the hot sauce in the refrigerator. It will continue to ferment slowly, developing more flavor over time.

Enjoy the rich and complex flavor of your homemade Fermented Black Garlic Hot Sauce!

Adjust the amount of garlic, brown sugar, or salt according to your taste preferences.

Cranberry and Jalapeno Fermented Hot Sauce

Ingredients:

- 2 cups fresh cranberries
- 5-6 fresh jalapeno peppers, stemmed and chopped
- 4 cloves garlic, peeled
- 1 tablespoon sea salt
- 1 tablespoon sugar (optional, for balance)
- 2 cups filtered water (chlorine-free)

Equipment:

- Blender or food processor
- Glass fermentation jar or airtight container
- Fermentation weight or a small glass jar to weigh down ingredients
- Cheesecloth or coffee filter
- Rubber band or string

Instructions:

Prep Ingredients: Rinse the cranberries and jalapenos under cold water. Remove the stems from the jalapenos and chop them roughly. Peel the garlic cloves.
Blend Ingredients: In a blender or food processor, combine the cranberries, jalapenos, garlic, sea salt, and sugar (if using). Pulse until you achieve a coarse mixture.
Transfer to Jar: Pour the blended mixture into a clean glass fermentation jar or airtight container. Press it down with a spoon to eliminate any air pockets.
Fermentation: Add enough filtered water to cover the mixture completely, leaving about an inch of space at the top of the jar. Place a fermentation weight or a small glass jar on top of the mixture to keep it submerged under the brine.
Cover and Secure: Cover the jar with a cheesecloth or a coffee filter and secure it with a rubber band or string. This allows airflow while keeping out contaminants.
Ferment: Place the jar in a cool, dark place, away from direct sunlight, and let it ferment for about 1 to 2 weeks. Check the hot sauce every few days to ensure that the mixture remains submerged and no mold forms on the surface. If mold appears, scoop it out immediately.
Taste Test: After 1 to 2 weeks, taste the hot sauce to check if it has developed the desired flavor. If it's tangy and fermented to your liking, proceed to the next step. If not, let it ferment for a few more days, tasting periodically.

Blend Again: Once fermented to your preference, remove the weight and cheesecloth. Use a clean spoon to taste the hot sauce again and adjust the seasoning if necessary. If you prefer a smoother texture, blend the mixture once more until smooth.
Bottle and Store: Transfer the hot sauce to clean, sterilized bottles or jars. Store it in the refrigerator for up to several months.

Enjoy your homemade cranberry and jalapeno fermented hot sauce as a condiment for tacos, grilled meats, or anything else that could use a flavorful kick! Adjust the amount of jalapenos to control the level of spiciness according to your preference.

Fermented Trinidad Moruga Scorpion Hot Sauce

Ingredients:

- 10-12 Trinidad Moruga Scorpion peppers (or adjust to your preferred heat level)
- 4 cloves garlic, peeled
- 1 small onion, chopped
- 2 carrots, peeled and chopped
- 1 tablespoon sea salt
- 2 cups filtered water (chlorine-free)
- Optional: additional spices such as cumin, coriander, or smoked paprika for added flavor

Equipment:

- Blender or food processor
- Glass fermentation jar or airtight container
- Fermentation weight or a small glass jar to weigh down ingredients
- Cheesecloth or coffee filter
- Rubber band or string

Instructions:

Prep Ingredients: Wear gloves to handle the Trinidad Moruga Scorpion peppers to avoid irritation. Rinse the peppers, remove the stems, and roughly chop them. Peel the garlic cloves and chop the onion and carrots.

Blend Ingredients: In a blender or food processor, combine the chopped peppers, garlic, onion, carrots, sea salt, and any optional spices you're using. Pulse until you achieve a coarse mixture.

Transfer to Jar: Pour the blended mixture into a clean glass fermentation jar or airtight container. Press it down with a spoon to eliminate any air pockets.

Fermentation: Add enough filtered water to cover the mixture completely, leaving about an inch of space at the top of the jar. Place a fermentation weight or a small glass jar on top of the mixture to keep it submerged under the brine.

Cover and Secure: Cover the jar with a cheesecloth or a coffee filter and secure it with a rubber band or string. This allows airflow while keeping out contaminants.

Ferment: Place the jar in a cool, dark place, away from direct sunlight, and let it ferment for about 1 to 2 weeks. Check the hot sauce every few days to ensure that the mixture remains submerged and no mold forms on the surface. If mold appears, scoop it out immediately.

Taste Test: After 1 to 2 weeks, taste the hot sauce to check if it has developed the desired flavor. If it's tangy and fermented to your liking, proceed to the next step. If not, let it ferment for a few more days, tasting periodically.
Blend Again: Once fermented to your preference, remove the weight and cheesecloth. Use a clean spoon to taste the hot sauce again and adjust the seasoning if necessary. If you prefer a smoother texture, blend the mixture once more until smooth.
Bottle and Store: Transfer the hot sauce to clean, sterilized bottles or jars. Store it in the refrigerator for up to several months.

Be cautious when handling Trinidad Moruga Scorpion peppers, as they are extremely hot. Adjust the quantity according to your heat tolerance. Enjoy your homemade fermented Trinidad Moruga Scorpion hot sauce with caution, as it packs a serious punch!

Peach and Habanero Fermented Hot Sauce

Ingredients:

- 4-5 ripe peaches, pitted and chopped
- 4-5 habanero peppers, stemmed and chopped (adjust quantity for desired heat level)
- 4 cloves garlic, peeled
- 1 tablespoon sea salt
- 2 cups filtered water (chlorine-free)

Equipment:

- Blender or food processor
- Glass fermentation jar or airtight container
- Fermentation weight or a small glass jar to weigh down ingredients
- Cheesecloth or coffee filter
- Rubber band or string

Instructions:

Prep Ingredients: Wash the peaches and habanero peppers thoroughly. Remove the pits from the peaches and chop them roughly. Wear gloves when handling habanero peppers to avoid irritation. Stem the peppers and chop them.

Blend Ingredients: In a blender or food processor, combine the chopped peaches, habanero peppers, garlic cloves, and sea salt. Pulse until you achieve a smooth mixture.

Transfer to Jar: Pour the blended mixture into a clean glass fermentation jar or airtight container. Press it down with a spoon to eliminate any air pockets.

Fermentation: Add enough filtered water to cover the mixture completely, leaving about an inch of space at the top of the jar. Place a fermentation weight or a small glass jar on top of the mixture to keep it submerged under the brine.

Cover and Secure: Cover the jar with a cheesecloth or a coffee filter and secure it with a rubber band or string. This allows airflow while keeping out contaminants.

Ferment: Place the jar in a cool, dark place, away from direct sunlight, and let it ferment for about 1 to 2 weeks. Check the hot sauce every few days to ensure that the mixture remains submerged and no mold forms on the surface. If mold appears, scoop it out immediately.

Taste Test: After 1 to 2 weeks, taste the hot sauce to check if it has developed the desired flavor. If it's tangy and fermented to your liking, proceed to the next step. If not, let it ferment for a few more days, tasting periodically.
Blend Again: Once fermented to your preference, remove the weight and cheesecloth. Use a clean spoon to taste the hot sauce again and adjust the seasoning if necessary. If you prefer a smoother texture, blend the mixture once more until smooth.
Bottle and Store: Transfer the hot sauce to clean, sterilized bottles or jars. Store it in the refrigerator for up to several months.

Enjoy your homemade peach and habanero fermented hot sauce as a spicy addition to your favorite dishes! Adjust the quantity of habanero peppers according to your heat preference.

Fermented Green Tomato Hot Sauce

Ingredients:

- 2 lbs green tomatoes, chopped
- 2-3 jalapeño peppers, stemmed and chopped (adjust quantity for desired heat level)
- 2 cloves garlic, peeled
- 1 small onion, chopped
- 1 tablespoon sea salt
- 2 cups filtered water (chlorine-free)

Equipment:

- Blender or food processor
- Glass fermentation jar or airtight container
- Fermentation weight or a small glass jar to weigh down ingredients
- Cheesecloth or coffee filter
- Rubber band or string

Instructions:

Prep Ingredients: Wash the green tomatoes, jalapeño peppers, garlic, and onion thoroughly. Remove any stems and chop them into smaller pieces.

Blend Ingredients: In a blender or food processor, combine the chopped green tomatoes, jalapeño peppers, garlic, onion, and sea salt. Pulse until you achieve a coarse mixture.

Transfer to Jar: Pour the blended mixture into a clean glass fermentation jar or airtight container. Press it down with a spoon to eliminate any air pockets.

Fermentation: Add enough filtered water to cover the mixture completely, leaving about an inch of space at the top of the jar. Place a fermentation weight or a small glass jar on top of the mixture to keep it submerged under the brine.

Cover and Secure: Cover the jar with a cheesecloth or a coffee filter and secure it with a rubber band or string. This allows airflow while keeping out contaminants.

Ferment: Place the jar in a cool, dark place, away from direct sunlight, and let it ferment for about 5 to 7 days. Check the hot sauce every day to ensure that the mixture remains submerged and no mold forms on the surface. If mold appears, scoop it out immediately.

Taste Test: After 5 to 7 days, taste the hot sauce to check if it has developed the desired flavor. If it's tangy and fermented to your liking, proceed to the next step. If not, let it ferment for a few more days, tasting periodically.
Blend Again: Once fermented to your preference, remove the weight and cheesecloth. Use a clean spoon to taste the hot sauce again and adjust the seasoning if necessary. If you prefer a smoother texture, blend the mixture once more until smooth.
Bottle and Store: Transfer the hot sauce to clean, sterilized bottles or jars. Store it in the refrigerator for up to several months.

Enjoy your homemade fermented green tomato hot sauce as a zesty addition to tacos, eggs, grilled meats, and more! Adjust the quantity of jalapeño peppers according to your heat preference.

Fermented Onion and Garlic Hot Sauce

Ingredients:

- 2 large onions, roughly chopped
- 1 head of garlic, cloves separated and peeled
- 2-3 jalapeño peppers, stemmed and chopped (adjust quantity for desired heat level)
- 1 tablespoon sea salt
- 2 cups filtered water (chlorine-free)

Equipment:

- Blender or food processor
- Glass fermentation jar or airtight container
- Fermentation weight or a small glass jar to weigh down ingredients
- Cheesecloth or coffee filter
- Rubber band or string

Instructions:

Prep Ingredients: Peel and chop the onions, separate and peel the garlic cloves, and chop the jalapeño peppers.

Blend Ingredients: In a blender or food processor, combine the chopped onions, garlic cloves, jalapeño peppers, sea salt, and a splash of filtered water. Pulse until you achieve a coarse mixture.

Transfer to Jar: Pour the blended mixture into a clean glass fermentation jar or airtight container. Press it down with a spoon to eliminate any air pockets.

Fermentation: Add enough filtered water to cover the mixture completely, leaving about an inch of space at the top of the jar. Place a fermentation weight or a small glass jar on top of the mixture to keep it submerged under the brine.

Cover and Secure: Cover the jar with a cheesecloth or a coffee filter and secure it with a rubber band or string. This allows airflow while keeping out contaminants.

Ferment: Place the jar in a cool, dark place, away from direct sunlight, and let it ferment for about 5 to 7 days. Check the hot sauce every day to ensure that the mixture remains submerged and no mold forms on the surface. If mold appears, scoop it out immediately.

Taste Test: After 5 to 7 days, taste the hot sauce to check if it has developed the desired flavor. If it's tangy and fermented to your liking, proceed to the next step. If not, let it ferment for a few more days, tasting periodically.

Blend Again: Once fermented to your preference, remove the weight and cheesecloth. Use a clean spoon to taste the hot sauce again and adjust the seasoning if necessary. If you prefer a smoother texture, blend the mixture once more until smooth.
Bottle and Store: Transfer the hot sauce to clean, sterilized bottles or jars. Store it in the refrigerator for up to several months.

Enjoy your homemade fermented onion and garlic hot sauce as a flavorful addition to soups, stews, sandwiches, and more! Adjust the quantity of jalapeño peppers according to your heat preference.

Blueberry and Ghost Pepper Fermented Hot Sauce

Ingredients:

- 2 cups fresh blueberries
- 3-4 ghost peppers (adjust quantity for desired heat level)
- 4 cloves garlic, peeled
- 1 tablespoon sea salt
- 2 cups filtered water (chlorine-free)

Equipment:

- Blender or food processor
- Glass fermentation jar or airtight container
- Fermentation weight or a small glass jar to weigh down ingredients
- Cheesecloth or coffee filter
- Rubber band or string

Instructions:

Prep Ingredients: Rinse the blueberries and ghost peppers. Remove the stems from the ghost peppers and chop them roughly. Peel the garlic cloves.

Blend Ingredients: In a blender or food processor, combine the blueberries, ghost peppers, garlic cloves, sea salt, and a splash of filtered water. Blend until you achieve a smooth mixture.

Transfer to Jar: Pour the blended mixture into a clean glass fermentation jar or airtight container. Press it down with a spoon to eliminate any air pockets.

Fermentation: Add enough filtered water to cover the mixture completely, leaving about an inch of space at the top of the jar. Place a fermentation weight or a small glass jar on top of the mixture to keep it submerged under the brine.

Cover and Secure: Cover the jar with a cheesecloth or a coffee filter and secure it with a rubber band or string. This allows airflow while keeping out contaminants.

Ferment: Place the jar in a cool, dark place, away from direct sunlight, and let it ferment for about 1 to 2 weeks. Check the hot sauce every few days to ensure that the mixture remains submerged and no mold forms on the surface. If mold appears, scoop it out immediately.

Taste Test: After 1 to 2 weeks, taste the hot sauce to check if it has developed the desired flavor. If it's tangy and fermented to your liking, proceed to the next step. If not, let it ferment for a few more days, tasting periodically.

Blend Again: Once fermented to your preference, remove the weight and cheesecloth. Use a clean spoon to taste the hot sauce again and adjust the seasoning if necessary. If you prefer a smoother texture, blend the mixture once more until smooth.
Bottle and Store: Transfer the hot sauce to clean, sterilized bottles or jars. Store it in the refrigerator for up to several months.

Enjoy your homemade blueberry and ghost pepper fermented hot sauce as a spicy and fruity addition to your favorite dishes! Adjust the quantity of ghost peppers according to your heat preference.

Fermented Bell Pepper Hot Sauce

Ingredients:

- 4-5 large bell peppers (any color), seeded and chopped
- 2 cloves garlic, peeled
- 1 small onion, chopped
- 2-3 jalapeño peppers, stemmed and chopped (optional, for added heat)
- 1 tablespoon sea salt
- 2 cups filtered water (chlorine-free)

Equipment:

- Blender or food processor
- Glass fermentation jar or airtight container
- Fermentation weight or a small glass jar to weigh down ingredients
- Cheesecloth or coffee filter
- Rubber band or string

Instructions:

Prep Ingredients: Wash the bell peppers, garlic, and onion thoroughly. Remove the seeds from the bell peppers and chop them into smaller pieces. Peel the garlic cloves and chop the onion.

Blend Ingredients: In a blender or food processor, combine the chopped bell peppers, garlic, onion, jalapeño peppers (if using), sea salt, and a splash of filtered water. Blend until you achieve a smooth mixture.

Transfer to Jar: Pour the blended mixture into a clean glass fermentation jar or airtight container. Press it down with a spoon to eliminate any air pockets.

Fermentation: Add enough filtered water to cover the mixture completely, leaving about an inch of space at the top of the jar. Place a fermentation weight or a small glass jar on top of the mixture to keep it submerged under the brine.

Cover and Secure: Cover the jar with a cheesecloth or a coffee filter and secure it with a rubber band or string. This allows airflow while keeping out contaminants.

Ferment: Place the jar in a cool, dark place, away from direct sunlight, and let it ferment for about 5 to 7 days. Check the hot sauce every day to ensure that the mixture remains submerged and no mold forms on the surface. If mold appears, scoop it out immediately.

Taste Test: After 5 to 7 days, taste the hot sauce to check if it has developed the desired flavor. If it's tangy and fermented to your liking, proceed to the next step. If not, let it ferment for a few more days, tasting periodically.
Blend Again: Once fermented to your preference, remove the weight and cheesecloth. Use a clean spoon to taste the hot sauce again and adjust the seasoning if necessary. If you prefer a smoother texture, blend the mixture once more until smooth.
Bottle and Store: Transfer the hot sauce to clean, sterilized bottles or jars. Store it in the refrigerator for up to several months.

Enjoy your homemade fermented bell pepper hot sauce as a flavorful addition to sandwiches, salads, grilled meats, and more! Adjust the quantity of jalapeño peppers according to your heat preference.

Fermented Beetroot and Chili Hot Sauce

Ingredients:

- 2 large beetroots, peeled and diced
- 4-5 red chili peppers (such as Fresno or red jalapeños), stemmed and chopped (adjust quantity for desired heat level)
- 4 cloves garlic, peeled
- 1 tablespoon sea salt
- 2 cups filtered water (chlorine-free)

Equipment:

- Blender or food processor
- Glass fermentation jar or airtight container
- Fermentation weight or a small glass jar to weigh down ingredients
- Cheesecloth or coffee filter
- Rubber band or string

Instructions:

Prep Ingredients: Wash the beetroots and chili peppers thoroughly. Peel the beetroots and dice them into smaller pieces. Stem the chili peppers and chop them.

Blend Ingredients: In a blender or food processor, combine the diced beetroots, chopped chili peppers, garlic cloves, sea salt, and a splash of filtered water. Blend until you achieve a smooth mixture.

Transfer to Jar: Pour the blended mixture into a clean glass fermentation jar or airtight container. Press it down with a spoon to eliminate any air pockets.

Fermentation: Add enough filtered water to cover the mixture completely, leaving about an inch of space at the top of the jar. Place a fermentation weight or a small glass jar on top of the mixture to keep it submerged under the brine.

Cover and Secure: Cover the jar with a cheesecloth or a coffee filter and secure it with a rubber band or string. This allows airflow while keeping out contaminants.

Ferment: Place the jar in a cool, dark place, away from direct sunlight, and let it ferment for about 5 to 7 days. Check the hot sauce every day to ensure that the mixture remains submerged and no mold forms on the surface. If mold appears, scoop it out immediately.

Taste Test: After 5 to 7 days, taste the hot sauce to check if it has developed the desired flavor. If it's tangy and fermented to your liking, proceed to the next step. If not, let it ferment for a few more days, tasting periodically.
Blend Again: Once fermented to your preference, remove the weight and cheesecloth. Use a clean spoon to taste the hot sauce again and adjust the seasoning if necessary. If you prefer a smoother texture, blend the mixture once more until smooth.
Bottle and Store: Transfer the hot sauce to clean, sterilized bottles or jars. Store it in the refrigerator for up to several months.

Enjoy your homemade fermented beetroot and chili hot sauce as a flavorful addition to salads, sandwiches, roasted vegetables, and more! Adjust the quantity of chili peppers according to your heat preference.

Orange and Habanero Fermented Hot Sauce

Ingredients:

- 4 large oranges, juiced and zested
- 5-6 habanero peppers, stemmed and chopped (adjust quantity for desired heat level)
- 4 cloves garlic, peeled
- 1 tablespoon sea salt
- 2 cups filtered water (chlorine-free)

Equipment:

- Blender or food processor
- Glass fermentation jar or airtight container
- Fermentation weight or a small glass jar to weigh down ingredients
- Cheesecloth or coffee filter
- Rubber band or string

Instructions:

Prep Ingredients: Juice the oranges and zest the peel of one or two oranges. Stem and chop the habanero peppers. Peel the garlic cloves.

Blend Ingredients: In a blender or food processor, combine the orange juice, orange zest, chopped habanero peppers, garlic cloves, sea salt, and a splash of filtered water. Blend until you achieve a smooth mixture.

Transfer to Jar: Pour the blended mixture into a clean glass fermentation jar or airtight container. Press it down with a spoon to eliminate any air pockets.

Fermentation: Add enough filtered water to cover the mixture completely, leaving about an inch of space at the top of the jar. Place a fermentation weight or a small glass jar on top of the mixture to keep it submerged under the brine.

Cover and Secure: Cover the jar with a cheesecloth or a coffee filter and secure it with a rubber band or string. This allows airflow while keeping out contaminants.

Ferment: Place the jar in a cool, dark place, away from direct sunlight, and let it ferment for about 5 to 7 days. Check the hot sauce every day to ensure that the mixture remains submerged and no mold forms on the surface. If mold appears, scoop it out immediately.

Taste Test: After 5 to 7 days, taste the hot sauce to check if it has developed the desired flavor. If it's tangy and fermented to your liking, proceed to the next step. If not, let it ferment for a few more days, tasting periodically.

Blend Again: Once fermented to your preference, remove the weight and cheesecloth. Use a clean spoon to taste the hot sauce again and adjust the seasoning if necessary. If you prefer a smoother texture, blend the mixture once more until smooth.

Bottle and Store: Transfer the hot sauce to clean, sterilized bottles or jars. Store it in the refrigerator for up to several months.

Enjoy your homemade fermented orange and habanero hot sauce as a flavorful addition to tacos, grilled meats, stir-fries, and more! Adjust the quantity of habanero peppers according to your heat preference.

Fermented Lemon Pepper Hot Sauce

Ingredients:

- 1 pound hot peppers (such as jalapeno or serrano), stemmed
- Zest and juice of 2 lemons
- 4 cloves garlic, peeled
- 1 tablespoon whole black peppercorns
- 1 tablespoon sea salt
- 2 cups filtered water

Instructions:

Wash the hot peppers thoroughly and remove the stems.
In a clean glass jar or fermentation crock, combine the hot peppers, lemon zest, lemon juice, garlic cloves, and whole black peppercorns.
Dissolve sea salt in filtered water to create a brine solution.
Pour the brine solution over the pepper mixture until they are fully submerged. Ensure there's at least an inch of space between the top of the mixture and the rim of the jar.
Place a fermentation weight on top of the mixture to keep everything submerged under the brine.
Cover the jar with a lid or a cloth secured with a rubber band to allow gases to escape while preventing dust and insects from entering.
Place the jar in a cool, dark area away from direct sunlight and let it ferment for about 1-2 weeks. Check the fermentation progress daily and skim off any mold that may form on the surface.
Once the fermentation is complete and the peppers have softened, transfer the contents of the jar to a blender or food processor.
Blend the mixture until smooth.
Strain the blended mixture through a fine-mesh sieve to remove any solids, if desired.
Transfer the strained hot sauce to clean glass bottles or jars for storage.
Seal the bottles or jars and store the hot sauce in the refrigerator. It will continue to ferment slowly, developing more flavor over time.

Enjoy the zesty and spicy flavor of your homemade Fermented Lemon Pepper Hot Sauce! Adjust the amount of garlic, lemon, or black peppercorns according to your taste preferences.

Pineapple and Jalapeno Fermented Hot Sauce

Ingredients:

- 1 pound jalapeño peppers, stemmed
- 2 cups fresh pineapple chunks
- 4 cloves garlic, peeled
- 1 tablespoon sea salt
- 2 cups filtered water

Instructions:

Wash the jalapeño peppers thoroughly and remove the stems.
In a clean glass jar or fermentation crock, combine the jalapeño peppers, pineapple chunks, and garlic cloves.
Dissolve sea salt in filtered water to create a brine solution.
Pour the brine solution over the pepper and pineapple mixture until they are fully submerged. Ensure there's at least an inch of space between the top of the mixture and the rim of the jar.
Place a fermentation weight on top of the mixture to keep everything submerged under the brine.
Cover the jar with a lid or a cloth secured with a rubber band to allow gases to escape while preventing dust and insects from entering.
Place the jar in a cool, dark area away from direct sunlight and let it ferment for about 1-2 weeks. Check the fermentation progress daily and skim off any mold that may form on the surface.
Once the fermentation is complete and the peppers have softened, transfer the contents of the jar to a blender or food processor.
Blend the mixture until smooth.
Strain the blended mixture through a fine-mesh sieve to remove any solids, if desired.
Transfer the strained hot sauce to clean glass bottles or jars for storage.
Seal the bottles or jars and store the hot sauce in the refrigerator. It will continue to ferment slowly, developing more flavor over time.

Enjoy the sweet and spicy flavor of your homemade Pineapple and Jalapeño Fermented

Hot Sauce! Adjust the amount of garlic or salt according to your taste preferences.

Fermented Carrot and Ginger Hot Sauce

Ingredients:

- 1 pound carrots, peeled and chopped
- 2 tablespoons grated fresh ginger
- 4 cloves garlic, peeled
- 1 tablespoon sea salt
- 2 cups filtered water
- 1-2 hot peppers (optional, for added heat)

Instructions:

In a clean glass jar or fermentation crock, combine the chopped carrots, grated ginger, and garlic cloves.

If desired, add 1-2 hot peppers to the mixture for added heat.

Dissolve sea salt in filtered water to create a brine solution.

Pour the brine solution over the carrot mixture until they are fully submerged.

Ensure there's at least an inch of space between the top of the mixture and the rim of the jar.

Place a fermentation weight on top of the mixture to keep everything submerged under the brine.

Cover the jar with a lid or a cloth secured with a rubber band to allow gases to escape while preventing dust and insects from entering.

Place the jar in a cool, dark area away from direct sunlight and let it ferment for about 1-2 weeks. Check the fermentation progress daily and skim off any mold that may form on the surface.

Once the fermentation is complete and the carrots have softened, transfer the contents of the jar to a blender or food processor.

Blend the mixture until smooth.

Strain the blended mixture through a fine-mesh sieve to remove any solids, if desired.

Transfer the strained hot sauce to clean glass bottles or jars for storage.

Seal the bottles or jars and store the hot sauce in the refrigerator. It will continue to ferment slowly, developing more flavor over time.

Enjoy the vibrant and spicy flavor of your homemade Fermented Carrot and Ginger Hot Sauce! Adjust the amount of ginger or hot peppers according to your taste preferences.

Cranberry and Ghost Pepper Fermented Hot Sauce

Ingredients:

- 1 pound cranberries
- 2-3 ghost peppers (adjust to taste), stemmed
- 4 cloves garlic, peeled
- 1 tablespoon sea salt
- 2 cups filtered water

Instructions:

Rinse the cranberries thoroughly and remove any stems.
In a clean glass jar or fermentation crock, combine the cranberries, ghost peppers, and garlic cloves.
Dissolve sea salt in filtered water to create a brine solution.
Pour the brine solution over the cranberry mixture until everything is fully submerged. Leave about an inch of space between the top of the mixture and the rim of the jar.
Place a fermentation weight on top to keep all the ingredients submerged under the brine.
Cover the jar with a lid or a cloth secured with a rubber band to allow gases to escape while preventing dust and insects from entering.
Place the jar in a cool, dark area away from direct sunlight and let it ferment for about 1-2 weeks. Check the fermentation progress daily and remove any mold that may form on the surface.
Once the fermentation is complete and the cranberries have softened, transfer the contents of the jar to a blender or food processor.
Blend the mixture until smooth.
Strain the blended mixture through a fine-mesh sieve to remove any solids, if desired.
Transfer the strained hot sauce to clean glass bottles or jars for storage.
Seal the bottles or jars and store the hot sauce in the refrigerator. It will continue to ferment slowly, developing more flavor over time.

Enjoy the unique combination of tart cranberries and intense heat from ghost peppers in your homemade Fermented Cranberry and Ghost Pepper Hot Sauce! Adjust the number of ghost peppers based on your preference for heat level.

Fermented Cherry Bomb Hot Sauce

Ingredients:

- 1 pound cherry bomb peppers, stemmed
- 4 cloves garlic, peeled
- 1 tablespoon sea salt
- 2 cups filtered water

Instructions:

Wash the cherry bomb peppers thoroughly and remove the stems.
In a clean glass jar or fermentation crock, combine the cherry bomb peppers and garlic cloves.
Dissolve sea salt in filtered water to create a brine solution.
Pour the brine solution over the pepper mixture until they are fully submerged.
Ensure there's at least an inch of space between the top of the mixture and the rim of the jar.
Place a fermentation weight on top of the mixture to keep everything submerged under the brine.
Cover the jar with a lid or a cloth secured with a rubber band to allow gases to escape while preventing dust and insects from entering.
Place the jar in a cool, dark area away from direct sunlight and let it ferment for about 1-2 weeks. Check the fermentation progress daily and skim off any mold that may form on the surface.
Once the fermentation is complete and the peppers have softened, transfer the contents of the jar to a blender or food processor.
Blend the mixture until smooth.
Strain the blended mixture through a fine-mesh sieve to remove any solids, if desired.
Transfer the strained hot sauce to clean glass bottles or jars for storage.
Seal the bottles or jars and store the hot sauce in the refrigerator. It will continue to ferment slowly, developing more flavor over time.

Enjoy the fiery flavor of your homemade Fermented Cherry Bomb Hot Sauce! Adjust the amount of garlic or salt according to your taste preferences.

Fermented Scotch Bonnet and Mango Hot Sauce

Ingredients:

- 1 pound Scotch Bonnet peppers, stemmed
- 2 ripe mangoes, peeled and diced
- 4 cloves garlic, peeled
- 1 tablespoon sea salt
- 2 cups filtered water

Instructions:

Wash the Scotch Bonnet peppers thoroughly and remove the stems.

In a clean glass jar or fermentation crock, combine the Scotch Bonnet peppers, diced mangoes, and garlic cloves.

Dissolve sea salt in filtered water to create a brine solution.

Pour the brine solution over the pepper and mango mixture until they are fully submerged. Ensure there's at least an inch of space between the top of the mixture and the rim of the jar.

Place a fermentation weight on top of the mixture to keep everything submerged under the brine.

Cover the jar with a lid or a cloth secured with a rubber band to allow gases to escape while preventing dust and insects from entering.

Place the jar in a cool, dark area away from direct sunlight and let it ferment for about 1-2 weeks. Check the fermentation progress daily and skim off any mold that may form on the surface.

Once the fermentation is complete and the peppers have softened, transfer the contents of the jar to a blender or food processor.

Blend the mixture until smooth.

Strain the blended mixture through a fine-mesh sieve to remove any solids, if desired.

Transfer the strained hot sauce to clean glass bottles or jars for storage.

Seal the bottles or jars and store the hot sauce in the refrigerator. It will continue to ferment slowly, developing more flavor over time.

Enjoy the tropical and spicy flavor of your homemade Fermented Scotch Bonnet and Mango Hot Sauce! Adjust the amount of garlic or salt according to your taste preferences.

Fermented Watermelon Hot Sauce

Ingredients:

- 4 cups diced watermelon (seedless)
- 2-3 hot peppers (such as jalapeño or serrano), stemmed and sliced
- 4 cloves garlic, peeled
- 1 tablespoon sea salt
- 2 cups filtered water

Instructions:

In a clean glass jar or fermentation crock, combine the diced watermelon, sliced hot peppers, and garlic cloves.

Dissolve sea salt in filtered water to create a brine solution.

Pour the brine solution over the watermelon mixture until they are fully submerged. Ensure there's at least an inch of space between the top of the mixture and the rim of the jar.

Place a fermentation weight on top of the mixture to keep everything submerged under the brine.

Cover the jar with a lid or a cloth secured with a rubber band to allow gases to escape while preventing dust and insects from entering.

Place the jar in a cool, dark area away from direct sunlight and let it ferment for about 1-2 weeks. Check the fermentation progress daily and skim off any mold that may form on the surface.

Once the fermentation is complete and the watermelon has softened, transfer the contents of the jar to a blender or food processor.

Blend the mixture until smooth.

Strain the blended mixture through a fine-mesh sieve to remove any solids, if desired.

Transfer the strained hot sauce to clean glass bottles or jars for storage.

Seal the bottles or jars and store the hot sauce in the refrigerator. It will continue to ferment slowly, developing more flavor over time.

Enjoy the refreshing and spicy flavor of your homemade Fermented Watermelon Hot Sauce! Adjust the amount of hot peppers or garlic according to your taste preferences.

Fermented Avocado and Jalapeno Hot Sauce

Ingredients:

- 2 ripe avocados, peeled and pitted
- 4-5 jalapeño peppers, stemmed and sliced
- 4 cloves garlic, peeled
- 1 tablespoon sea salt
- 2 cups filtered water

Instructions:

In a clean glass jar or fermentation crock, combine the peeled and pitted avocados, sliced jalapeño peppers, and garlic cloves.

Dissolve sea salt in filtered water to create a brine solution.

Pour the brine solution over the avocado mixture until they are fully submerged. Ensure there's at least an inch of space between the top of the mixture and the rim of the jar.

Place a fermentation weight on top of the mixture to keep everything submerged under the brine.

Cover the jar with a lid or a cloth secured with a rubber band to allow gases to escape while preventing dust and insects from entering.

Place the jar in a cool, dark area away from direct sunlight and let it ferment for about 1-2 weeks. Check the fermentation progress daily and skim off any mold that may form on the surface.

Once the fermentation is complete and the avocados have softened, transfer the contents of the jar to a blender or food processor.

Blend the mixture until smooth.

Strain the blended mixture through a fine-mesh sieve to remove any solids, if desired.

Transfer the strained hot sauce to clean glass bottles or jars for storage.

Seal the bottles or jars and store the hot sauce in the refrigerator. It will continue to ferment slowly, developing more flavor over time.

Enjoy the creamy texture and spicy flavor of your homemade Fermented Avocado and Jalapeño Hot Sauce! Adjust the amount of jalapeño peppers or garlic according to your taste preferences.

Fermented Pineapple and Papaya Hot Sauce

Ingredients:

- 2 cups diced pineapple
- 2 cups diced papaya
- 4 cloves garlic, peeled
- 1 tablespoon sea salt
- 2 cups filtered water
- 2-3 hot peppers (such as jalapeño or habanero), stemmed and sliced (optional, for heat)

Instructions:

In a clean glass jar or fermentation crock, combine the diced pineapple, diced papaya, and garlic cloves.
If you desire heat, add the sliced hot peppers to the mixture.
Dissolve sea salt in filtered water to create a brine solution.
Pour the brine solution over the fruit mixture until they are fully submerged.
Ensure there's at least an inch of space between the top of the mixture and the rim of the jar.
Place a fermentation weight on top of the mixture to keep everything submerged under the brine.
Cover the jar with a lid or a cloth secured with a rubber band to allow gases to escape while preventing dust and insects from entering.
Place the jar in a cool, dark area away from direct sunlight and let it ferment for about 1-2 weeks. Check the fermentation progress daily and skim off any mold that may form on the surface.
Once the fermentation is complete and the fruit has softened, transfer the contents of the jar to a blender or food processor.
Blend the mixture until smooth.
Strain the blended mixture through a fine-mesh sieve to remove any solids, if desired.
Transfer the strained hot sauce to clean glass bottles or jars for storage.
Seal the bottles or jars and store the hot sauce in the refrigerator. It will continue to ferment slowly, developing more flavor over time.

Enjoy the tropical flavor of your homemade Fermented Pineapple and Papaya Hot Sauce! Adjust the amount of hot peppers or garlic according to your taste preferences.

Fermented Cranberry and Jalapeno Hot Sauce

Ingredients:

- 2 cups fresh or frozen cranberries
- 4-5 jalapeño peppers, stemmed and sliced
- 4 cloves garlic, peeled
- 1 tablespoon sea salt
- 2 cups filtered water

Instructions:

Rinse the cranberries thoroughly and remove any stems.

In a clean glass jar or fermentation crock, combine the cranberries, sliced jalapeño peppers, and garlic cloves.

Dissolve sea salt in filtered water to create a brine solution.

Pour the brine solution over the cranberry mixture until they are fully submerged. Ensure there's at least an inch of space between the top of the mixture and the rim of the jar.

Place a fermentation weight on top of the mixture to keep everything submerged under the brine.

Cover the jar with a lid or a cloth secured with a rubber band to allow gases to escape while preventing dust and insects from entering.

Place the jar in a cool, dark area away from direct sunlight and let it ferment for about 1-2 weeks. Check the fermentation progress daily and skim off any mold that may form on the surface.

Once the fermentation is complete and the cranberries have softened, transfer the contents of the jar to a blender or food processor.

Blend the mixture until smooth.

Strain the blended mixture through a fine-mesh sieve to remove any solids, if desired.

Transfer the strained hot sauce to clean glass bottles or jars for storage.

Seal the bottles or jars and store the hot sauce in the refrigerator. It will continue to ferment slowly, developing more flavor over time.

Enjoy the sweet and spicy flavor of your homemade Fermented Cranberry and Jalapeño Hot Sauce! Adjust the amount of jalapeño peppers or garlic according to your taste preferences.

Fermented Mango and Pineapple Hot Sauce

Ingredients:

- 2 cups diced mango
- 2 cups diced pineapple
- 4 cloves garlic, peeled
- 1 tablespoon sea salt
- 2 cups filtered water
- 2-3 hot peppers (such as jalapeño or habanero), stemmed and sliced (optional, for heat)

Instructions:

In a clean glass jar or fermentation crock, combine the diced mango, diced pineapple, and garlic cloves.
If you desire heat, add the sliced hot peppers to the mixture.
Dissolve sea salt in filtered water to create a brine solution.
Pour the brine solution over the fruit mixture until they are fully submerged.
Ensure there's at least an inch of space between the top of the mixture and the rim of the jar.
Place a fermentation weight on top of the mixture to keep everything submerged under the brine.
Cover the jar with a lid or a cloth secured with a rubber band to allow gases to escape while preventing dust and insects from entering.
Place the jar in a cool, dark area away from direct sunlight and let it ferment for about 1-2 weeks. Check the fermentation progress daily and skim off any mold that may form on the surface.
Once the fermentation is complete and the fruit has softened, transfer the contents of the jar to a blender or food processor.
Blend the mixture until smooth.
Strain the blended mixture through a fine-mesh sieve to remove any solids, if desired.
Transfer the strained hot sauce to clean glass bottles or jars for storage.
Seal the bottles or jars and store the hot sauce in the refrigerator. It will continue to ferment slowly, developing more flavor over time.

Enjoy the tropical flavor of your homemade Fermented Mango and Pineapple Hot Sauce! Adjust the amount of hot peppers or garlic according to your taste preferences.

Fermented Strawberry and Habanero Hot Sauce

Ingredients:

- 2 cups diced strawberries
- 3-4 habanero peppers, stemmed and sliced
- 4 cloves garlic, peeled
- 1 tablespoon sea salt
- 2 cups filtered water

Instructions:

In a clean glass jar or fermentation crock, combine the diced strawberries, sliced habanero peppers, and garlic cloves.

Dissolve sea salt in filtered water to create a brine solution.

Pour the brine solution over the strawberry mixture until they are fully submerged. Ensure there's at least an inch of space between the top of the mixture and the rim of the jar.

Place a fermentation weight on top of the mixture to keep everything submerged under the brine.

Cover the jar with a lid or a cloth secured with a rubber band to allow gases to escape while preventing dust and insects from entering.

Place the jar in a cool, dark area away from direct sunlight and let it ferment for about 1-2 weeks. Check the fermentation progress daily and skim off any mold that may form on the surface.

Once the fermentation is complete and the strawberries have softened, transfer the contents of the jar to a blender or food processor.

Blend the mixture until smooth.

Strain the blended mixture through a fine-mesh sieve to remove any solids, if desired.

Transfer the strained hot sauce to clean glass bottles or jars for storage.

Seal the bottles or jars and store the hot sauce in the refrigerator. It will continue to ferment slowly, developing more flavor over time.

Enjoy the sweet and spicy flavor of your homemade Fermented Strawberry and Habanero Hot Sauce! Adjust the amount of habanero peppers or garlic according to your taste preferences.

Fermented Tomato and Basil Hot Sauce

Ingredients:

- 2 cups chopped tomatoes
- 1 cup fresh basil leaves
- 4 cloves garlic, peeled
- 1 tablespoon sea salt
- 2 cups filtered water
- 2-3 hot peppers (such as jalapeño or serrano), stemmed and sliced (optional, for heat)

Instructions:

In a clean glass jar or fermentation crock, combine the chopped tomatoes, basil leaves, and garlic cloves.
If desired, add the sliced hot peppers to the mixture for added heat.
Dissolve sea salt in filtered water to create a brine solution.
Pour the brine solution over the tomato mixture until they are fully submerged.
Ensure there's at least an inch of space between the top of the mixture and the rim of the jar.
Place a fermentation weight on top of the mixture to keep everything submerged under the brine.
Cover the jar with a lid or a cloth secured with a rubber band to allow gases to escape while preventing dust and insects from entering.
Place the jar in a cool, dark area away from direct sunlight and let it ferment for about 1-2 weeks. Check the fermentation progress daily and skim off any mold that may form on the surface.
Once the fermentation is complete and the tomatoes have softened, transfer the contents of the jar to a blender or food processor.
Blend the mixture until smooth.
Strain the blended mixture through a fine-mesh sieve to remove any solids, if desired.
Transfer the strained hot sauce to clean glass bottles or jars for storage.
Seal the bottles or jars and store the hot sauce in the refrigerator. It will continue to ferment slowly, developing more flavor over time.

Enjoy the savory and herbaceous flavor of your homemade Fermented Tomato and Basil Hot Sauce! Adjust the amount of hot peppers or garlic according to your taste preferences.

Fermented Grapefruit and Ghost Pepper Hot Sauce

Ingredients:

- 4-5 ghost peppers (adjust according to your heat preference)
- 2 large grapefruits
- 4 cloves of garlic, minced
- 1 tablespoon sea salt
- 1 tablespoon sugar
- 1 cup water

Instructions:

Wear gloves when handling ghost peppers to avoid skin irritation. Remove the stems from the ghost peppers and roughly chop them.

Cut the grapefruits in half and juice them, reserving the juice in a bowl. You can also scoop out some of the pulp if desired.

In a clean glass jar, combine the chopped ghost peppers, grapefruit juice, minced garlic, sea salt, and sugar.

Add water to the jar until the ingredients are fully submerged. Make sure to leave some space at the top of the jar for fermentation gases to escape.

Seal the jar tightly and shake it gently to mix the ingredients.

Store the jar in a cool, dark place for about 1-2 weeks to ferment. Check the jar every day to release any built-up gases by slightly loosening the lid.

After the fermentation process is complete, use a blender or immersion blender to blend the mixture until smooth.

If the sauce is too thick, you can add a little water to reach your desired consistency.

Taste the sauce and adjust the seasoning if needed, adding more salt or sugar according to your preference.

Strain the sauce through a fine-mesh sieve to remove any remaining pulp or seeds, if desired.

Transfer the hot sauce to clean, sterilized bottles or jars for storage.

Refrigerate the hot sauce and use it as desired. The flavors will continue to develop over time.

Remember that ghost peppers are extremely spicy, so use caution when handling and consuming this hot sauce. Adjust the number of peppers to suit your heat tolerance. Enjoy experimenting with this unique and flavorful hot sauce!

Fermented Pineapple and Mango Hot Sauce

Ingredients:

- 2 cups diced pineapple
- 1 cup diced mango
- 4 cloves garlic, minced
- 1-2 habanero peppers (adjust to taste and desired spice level)
- 1 tablespoon sea salt
- 1 tablespoon sugar
- 1 cup water

Instructions:

Begin by preparing the fruits and vegetables. Peel and dice the pineapple and mango, mince the garlic, and remove the stems from the habanero peppers. You can adjust the number of habanero peppers depending on your spice preference.

In a clean glass jar, combine the diced pineapple, mango, minced garlic, habanero peppers, sea salt, and sugar.

Add water to the jar until all the ingredients are fully submerged. Leave some space at the top of the jar for fermentation gases to escape.

Seal the jar tightly and shake it gently to mix the ingredients.

Store the jar in a cool, dark place for about 1-2 weeks to ferment. Check the jar every day to release any built-up gases by slightly loosening the lid.

After the fermentation process is complete, use a blender or immersion blender to blend the mixture until smooth.

If the sauce is too thick, you can add a little water to reach your desired consistency.

Taste the sauce and adjust the seasoning if needed, adding more salt or sugar according to your preference.

Strain the sauce through a fine-mesh sieve to remove any remaining pulp or seeds, if desired.

Transfer the hot sauce to clean, sterilized bottles or jars for storage.

Refrigerate the hot sauce and use it as desired. The flavors will continue to develop over time.

This fermented pineapple and mango hot sauce will add a sweet and spicy kick to your favorite dishes. Enjoy experimenting with different flavor combinations and spice levels!

Fermented Kiwi and Jalapeno Hot Sauce

Ingredients:

- 4 kiwis, peeled and diced
- 4-5 jalapeno peppers, sliced (adjust according to your heat preference)
- 4 cloves garlic, minced
- 1 tablespoon sea salt
- 1 tablespoon sugar
- 1 cup water

Instructions:

Begin by preparing the fruits and vegetables. Peel the kiwis and dice them. Slice the jalapeno peppers, and mince the garlic.

In a clean glass jar, combine the diced kiwis, sliced jalapeno peppers, minced garlic, sea salt, and sugar.

Add water to the jar until all the ingredients are fully submerged. Leave some space at the top of the jar for fermentation gases to escape.

Seal the jar tightly and shake it gently to mix the ingredients.

Store the jar in a cool, dark place for about 1-2 weeks to ferment. Check the jar every day to release any built-up gases by slightly loosening the lid.

After the fermentation process is complete, use a blender or immersion blender to blend the mixture until smooth.

If the sauce is too thick, you can add a little water to reach your desired consistency.

Taste the sauce and adjust the seasoning if needed, adding more salt or sugar according to your preference.

Strain the sauce through a fine-mesh sieve to remove any remaining pulp or seeds, if desired.

Transfer the hot sauce to clean, sterilized bottles or jars for storage.

Refrigerate the hot sauce and use it as desired. The flavors will continue to develop over time.

This fermented kiwi and jalapeno hot sauce will add a delightful balance of sweetness and heat to your favorite dishes. Enjoy experimenting with this unique flavor combination!

Fermented Cherry and Ghost Pepper Hot Sauce

Ingredients:

- 2 cups pitted cherries
- 4-5 ghost peppers (adjust according to your heat preference)
- 4 cloves garlic, minced
- 1 tablespoon sea salt
- 1 tablespoon sugar
- 1 cup water

Instructions:

Start by preparing the ingredients. Pit the cherries and roughly chop them. Remove the stems from the ghost peppers and chop them as well. Wear gloves when handling ghost peppers to avoid skin irritation.

In a clean glass jar, combine the chopped cherries, chopped ghost peppers, minced garlic, sea salt, and sugar.

Add water to the jar until all the ingredients are fully submerged. Leave some space at the top of the jar for fermentation gases to escape.

Seal the jar tightly and shake it gently to mix the ingredients.

Store the jar in a cool, dark place for about 1-2 weeks to ferment. Check the jar every day to release any built-up gases by slightly loosening the lid.

After the fermentation process is complete, use a blender or immersion blender to blend the mixture until smooth.

If the sauce is too thick, you can add a little water to reach your desired consistency.

Taste the sauce and adjust the seasoning if needed, adding more salt or sugar according to your preference.

Strain the sauce through a fine-mesh sieve to remove any remaining pulp or seeds, if desired.

Transfer the hot sauce to clean, sterilized bottles or jars for storage.

Refrigerate the hot sauce and use it as desired. The flavors will continue to develop over time.

This fermented cherry and ghost pepper hot sauce will add a deliciously fruity and fiery kick to your favorite dishes. Enjoy experimenting with this unique flavor combination!

Fermented Blackberry and Habanero Hot Sauce

Ingredients:

- 2 cups blackberries
- 4-5 habanero peppers (adjust according to your heat preference)
- 4 cloves garlic, minced
- 1 tablespoon sea salt
- 1 tablespoon sugar
- 1 cup water

Instructions:

Start by preparing the ingredients. Rinse the blackberries and remove any stems. Remove the stems from the habanero peppers and chop them.

In a clean glass jar, combine the blackberries, chopped habanero peppers, minced garlic, sea salt, and sugar.

Add water to the jar until all the ingredients are fully submerged. Leave some space at the top of the jar for fermentation gases to escape.

Seal the jar tightly and shake it gently to mix the ingredients.

Store the jar in a cool, dark place for about 1-2 weeks to ferment. Check the jar every day to release any built-up gases by slightly loosening the lid.

After the fermentation process is complete, use a blender or immersion blender to blend the mixture until smooth.

If the sauce is too thick, you can add a little water to reach your desired consistency.

Taste the sauce and adjust the seasoning if needed, adding more salt or sugar according to your preference.

Strain the sauce through a fine-mesh sieve to remove any remaining pulp or seeds, if desired.

Transfer the hot sauce to clean, sterilized bottles or jars for storage.

Refrigerate the hot sauce and use it as desired. The flavors will continue to develop over time.

This fermented blackberry and habanero hot sauce will add a burst of fruity sweetness and fiery heat to your favorite dishes. Enjoy experimenting with this unique flavor combination!

Fermented Raspberry and Jalapeno Hot Sauce

Ingredients:

- 2 cups fresh raspberries
- 1 cup jalapeno peppers, chopped (adjust quantity based on desired heat level)
- 4 cloves garlic, minced
- 1 tablespoon sea salt
- 1 tablespoon honey or sugar (optional, for added sweetness)
- 1 cup water (non-chlorinated)
- 1/4 cup apple cider vinegar or white vinegar (to stop the fermentation process)

Instructions:

Prepare the Ingredients:
- Rinse raspberries and jalapenos thoroughly.
- Remove the stems from the jalapenos and chop them into small pieces. Wear gloves while handling jalapenos to protect your skin from the heat.
- Mince the garlic cloves.

Combine Ingredients:
- In a clean glass jar or fermentation vessel, layer the raspberries, jalapenos, garlic, sea salt, and honey (if using), ensuring an even distribution of ingredients.
- Pour the water over the ingredients, ensuring they are fully submerged. Leave some headspace in the jar to allow for fermentation gases to escape.

Fermentation Process:
- Cover the jar with a breathable cloth or fermenting lid to allow air circulation while keeping out contaminants.
- Place the jar in a cool, dark place, away from direct sunlight, and let it ferment for about 1-2 weeks. Check the jar every day to ensure the ingredients remain submerged under the brine. If necessary, use a weight to keep them submerged.
- During fermentation, you may notice bubbles forming, which is a sign that the fermentation process is active.

Check for Fermentation Completion:
- Taste the mixture after about a week to gauge its flavor and heat level. If it's to your liking, proceed to the next step. If not, allow it to ferment longer until it reaches the desired flavor.

Blending and Straining:

- Once fermentation is complete, use a blender or food processor to puree the mixture until smooth.
- If desired, strain the mixture through a fine-mesh sieve or cheesecloth to remove any solids, resulting in a smoother hot sauce.

Final Adjustments:

- Stir in the vinegar to halt the fermentation process and add tanginess to the sauce.
- Taste the hot sauce and adjust the seasoning if necessary, adding more salt or sweetener according to your preference.

Bottling and Storage:

- Transfer the hot sauce into sterilized bottles or jars, ensuring they are airtight.
- Store the hot sauce in the refrigerator for up to 6 months for optimal flavor and freshness.

Enjoy your homemade Fermented Raspberry and Jalapeno Hot Sauce drizzled over tacos, grilled meats, sandwiches, or any dish that could use a flavorful kick! Adjust the quantities of raspberries and jalapenos to suit your taste preferences and desired level of spiciness.

Fermented Apple and Cayenne Hot Sauce

Ingredients:

- 4 cups chopped apples (use a sweet variety like Fuji or Gala)
- 1 cup chopped cayenne peppers (adjust quantity based on desired heat level)
- 4 cloves garlic, minced
- 1 tablespoon sea salt
- 1 tablespoon honey or sugar (optional, for added sweetness)
- 1 cup water (non-chlorinated)
- 1/4 cup apple cider vinegar or white vinegar (to stop the fermentation process)

Instructions:

Prepare the Ingredients:
- Peel, core, and chop the apples into small pieces.
- Remove the stems from the cayenne peppers and chop them into small pieces. Consider wearing gloves while handling hot peppers to avoid skin irritation.
- Mince the garlic cloves.

Combine Ingredients:
- In a clean glass jar or fermentation vessel, layer the chopped apples, cayenne peppers, minced garlic, sea salt, and honey (if using), ensuring an even distribution of ingredients.
- Pour the water over the ingredients, ensuring they are fully submerged. Leave some headspace in the jar to allow for fermentation gases to escape.

Fermentation Process:
- Cover the jar with a breathable cloth or fermenting lid to allow air circulation while keeping out contaminants.
- Place the jar in a cool, dark place, away from direct sunlight, and let it ferment for about 1-2 weeks. Check the jar every day to ensure the ingredients remain submerged under the brine. Use a weight if necessary.
- During fermentation, you may notice bubbles forming, indicating that the fermentation process is active.

Check for Fermentation Completion:
- Taste the mixture after about a week to gauge its flavor and heat level. If it's to your liking, proceed to the next step. If not, allow it to ferment longer until it reaches the desired flavor.

Blending and Straining:

- Once fermentation is complete, use a blender or food processor to puree the mixture until smooth.
- If desired, strain the mixture through a fine-mesh sieve or cheesecloth to remove any solids, resulting in a smoother hot sauce.

Final Adjustments:

- Stir in the vinegar to halt the fermentation process and add tanginess to the sauce.
- Taste the hot sauce and adjust the seasoning if necessary, adding more salt or sweetener according to your preference.

Bottling and Storage:

- Transfer the hot sauce into sterilized bottles or jars, ensuring they are airtight.
- Store the hot sauce in the refrigerator for up to 6 months for optimal flavor and freshness.

This Fermented Apple and Cayenne Hot Sauce pairs well with a variety of dishes, adding a punch of flavor and heat. Adjust the quantities of apples and cayenne peppers to suit your taste preferences and desired level of spiciness. Enjoy experimenting with this homemade condiment!

Fermented Plum and Scotch Bonnet Hot Sauce

Ingredients:

- 2 cups ripe plums, pitted and chopped
- 1 cup Scotch Bonnet peppers, chopped (adjust quantity based on desired heat level)
- 4 cloves garlic, minced
- 1 tablespoon sea salt
- 1 tablespoon honey or sugar (optional, for added sweetness)
- 1 cup water (non-chlorinated)
- 1/4 cup apple cider vinegar or white vinegar (to stop the fermentation process)

Instructions:

Prepare the Ingredients:
- Pit and chop the ripe plums into small pieces.
- Remove the stems from the Scotch Bonnet peppers and chop them into small pieces. Be cautious when handling hot peppers and consider wearing gloves.
- Mince the garlic cloves.

Combine Ingredients:
- In a clean glass jar or fermentation vessel, layer the chopped plums, Scotch Bonnet peppers, minced garlic, sea salt, and honey (if using), ensuring an even distribution of ingredients.
- Pour the water over the ingredients, making sure they are fully submerged. Leave some headspace in the jar to allow for fermentation gases to escape.

Fermentation Process:
- Cover the jar with a breathable cloth or fermenting lid to allow air circulation while keeping out contaminants.
- Place the jar in a cool, dark place, away from direct sunlight, and let it ferment for about 1-2 weeks. Check the jar every day to ensure the ingredients remain submerged under the brine. Use a weight if necessary.
- During fermentation, you may notice bubbles forming, indicating that the fermentation process is active.

Check for Fermentation Completion:
- Taste the mixture after about a week to gauge its flavor and heat level. If it's to your liking, proceed to the next step. If not, allow it to ferment longer until it reaches the desired flavor.

Blending and Straining:

- Once fermentation is complete, use a blender or food processor to puree the mixture until smooth.
- If desired, strain the mixture through a fine-mesh sieve or cheesecloth to remove any solids, resulting in a smoother hot sauce.

Final Adjustments:

- Stir in the vinegar to halt the fermentation process and add tanginess to the sauce.
- Taste the hot sauce and adjust the seasoning if necessary, adding more salt or sweetener according to your preference.

Bottling and Storage:

- Transfer the hot sauce into sterilized bottles or jars, ensuring they are airtight.
- Store the hot sauce in the refrigerator for up to 6 months for optimal flavor and freshness.

This Fermented Plum and Scotch Bonnet Hot Sauce is perfect for adding a spicy kick to your favorite dishes. Adjust the quantities of plums and Scotch Bonnet peppers to suit your taste preferences and desired level of spiciness. Enjoy experimenting with this homemade condiment!

9 798869 265463